PINK
BLACKBIRDS

PINK BLACKBIRDS

evocative utterances of my mother

ROBERT J. ROWELL

ILLUSTRATIONS, DESIGN, AND BACKGROUND TEXT BY

SABETH IRELAND

PINK BLACKBIRDS
evocative utterances of my mother

J. G. Eastman | Art Deco Dog Publishing
P.O. Box 193
Moss Beach | CA | 94038
artdecodog@gmail.com

Ordering Information:
This book is available for purchase in the U.S. and internationally
through Ingram, online stores, and other retailers.

First Edition
Published by Art Deco Dog Publishing

ISBN 978-1-7323827-4-9 Hardcover
978-1-7323827-8-7 eBook

Printed in the United States of America

to my brother and sister, John and Kathy

— with a nod to Rose's recipe —

acknowledgements

My deep gratitude to my friend, collaborator, and brilliant illustrator Sabeth Ireland for her many contributions to this book. Without her, this book would not have been possible.

Special thanks to my sister, Kathy, for contributing our mother's quips I had forgotten and for her review of and suggestions for the book.

Many thanks to my friend Judi Eastman for her advice, assistance and guidance with book design and publication. Her insights and knowledge have been invaluable.

Background copy on the origins of popular slang and idioms were compiled from several learned sources online. Thanks to *The Phrase Finder* (phrases.org.uk), *Idiom Origins* (idiomorigins.org) and *The Urban Dictionary* (urbandictionary.com), among others, for their valuable knowledge.

My mother, Mary Moroney Rowell, was born in 1911 in Grafton, Massachusetts. She grew up in a house her grandfather built on Moroney Road in Grafton. She graduated from Framingham State Normal School (later Framingham State Teachers College) in 1929. Unfortunately, that year was the beginning of the Great Depression and teaching jobs were scarce. So she found work in various other areas.

During summers in high school and college she worked in a hat factory. That was likely the beginning of her lifelong interest in millinery. In later years she made custom hats for clients in the local community, always with her personal label sewn inside. She also taught millinery to adults in evening classes and was a guest on local television, talking about and showcasing her millinery. She occasionally traveled to Chicago, Illinois to stock up on supplies at Fox Millinery Supply, which were shipped back to our home.

My mother was also an accomplished baker. She made almost any baked goods you could think of, and there was often something freshly baked awaiting us kids when we came home from school. She particularly excelled at pies. Her flaky pie crust (made with lard, of course) was unequaled. She could roll out the crust for a two-crust pie in a flash. Leftover dough she made into "crusters." These were dough cut into strips, dusted with cinnamon and sugar, rolled up and brushed with egg wash, then baked. I might have liked those more than the pie.

My mother was at times rather formidable. She was no pushover. As long as I can remember, she had a saying or evocative quip, for most any occasion. Some were undoubtedly original while others were common to or adapted from her generation. I find myself using some of them more and more over the years. Perhaps you will too.

Enjoy!

GREAT EXPECTATIONS

giving oneself airs

"We'll be having wind sauce and wind pudding."

Offered as a response to "What's for dinner?," this saying apparently originated in Great Britain and thence to the colonies in North America and the West Indies. It has been used throughout history by mothers in times of deprivation and in the American Civil War as an option voiced by soldiers at the sight of a wild squirrel boiling in the cookpot. Variations include "air pie and windy pudding" and "air custard and wind pie."

You expect the earth and the pink fence.

variation: "...the earth and the picket fence."

God helps those who help themselves.

This is *not* the Waldorf Astoria!

We're living high— like pigs in the attic.

variation: "Living high on the hog."

OBSERVATIONS

don't say I said so, but...

"She's got more business than Eleanor Roosevelt."

He looks like he just stepped out of a bandbox.

She's none the worse for the wear.

She's the gossip of Grinder's Switch.

Most likely borrowed from Grand Ole Opry comedienne Minnie Pearl (1912-1996), whose fictional hometown was Grinder's Switch. In addition to "the gossip," Grinder's Switch was populated by characters "Uncle Nabob," his wife "Aunt Ambrosia," "Lucifer Hucklehead," and "Miss Lizzie Tinkum."

He bought it lock, stock, and barrel.

She's big as life and twice as natural.

If that wouldn't stop a clock, it would make it run backwards.

Occasionally whispered to me in church when my mother saw someone dressed outlandishly or in mismatched plaids.

He has more nerve than a brass monkey!

Setting aside for a moment the popular nautical attribution to this phrase's origin, its earliest use alluded to cold rather than nerve, as in "cold enough to freeze the (tail/nose/balls) off a brass monkey." The nautical explanation asserts that the balls were not monkey parts but iron cannonballs stored on the decks of British sailing vessels in a brass containment known as a monkey. Experts on the Age of Sail find this absurd on too many levels to mention here. The curious are invited to look it up and decide for themselves whether they believe it. Meanwhile, that frozen brass monkey could easily have become a *brassy* monkey ("brass" equalling "nerve"), *et voilà*!

He'd rather be despised than ignored.

One half of the world doesn't know how the other half lives.

That's a whole other ball of wax.

You've got that cockeyed and backwards.

She's one smart cookie.

There's no two ways about it.

He has a few loose screws.

She's a fussbudget.

You're putting the cart before the horse.

Save your breath to cool your soup.

In like Flynn.

If you suspect this expression has to do with the flamboyant, swashbuckling and swoon-inspiring actor of Hollywood's Golden Age, Errol Flynn, you are right! It refers specifically to Mr. Flynn's unfailing success at "romantic" encounters.

NONSENSE

idioms & miscellaneous cockamamia

" She's off her rocker. "

She's talking through her hat.

Who's cockamamie idea
was that?

Dumb as a doorbell.

Fools rush in where angels fear to tread.

That's a lot of malarkey.

The etymology of "malarkey" (meaningless talk, nonsense) is a mystery, but its use is attributed to American slang of the 1920s (see also "all wet," facing page). Synonyms for malarkey: bilge, bunkum, hooey, twaddle, claptrap, applesauce.

She's all wet.

Use your head for something
besides a hat rack.

She's got bats in the belfry.

UH OH

warning shots & trouble brewing

"She can stew in her own juices."

She'll change her tune.

I have a bone to pick with you.

It's dead as a doornail.

First found in poems of the 1300s, used later by William Shakespeare in the 1500s and later still by Charles Dickens in *A Christmas Carol*, 1843. It is thought to refer to the practice of securing doornails by "clenching" them. Clenching involves bending over the protruding end of the nail and hammering it into the wood. When a nail has been clenched, it has been "dead nailed" and is not easily brought back to life.

I'll fix her!

Run, don't walk, to the nearest exit.

He's in a lot of hot water.

I'm going to make mincemeat out of you!

TREAD SOFTLY

keep cool & don't rock the boat

"We're between the devil and the deep blue sea."

This phrase is yet another believed by many to be of nautical origin; the "devil" being the precarious seam where the ship's deck meets the hull, and the hapless sailor the one who has to caulk it from such an unreliable perch. However, there is little to back up this explanation, since the first in-print record of "the devil and the deep sea" is found quite early, in 1637, and there is no historical evidence that mariners were referring to the seam as a "devil" back then. More likely, users of this saying were describing the ever-undesirable choice between damnation and drowning.

Someone will
lower the boom.

You're skating on thin ice.

He's hell-bent for an election.

Don't upset the apple cart.

That's between you, me,
and the lamp post.

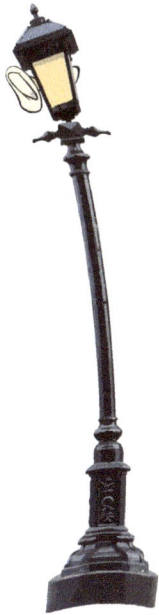

FRUSTRATION

faint cries from the edge

"The next time we do *that*, there'll be pink blackbirds on 4th Avenue."

Overheard upon the return home (to 4th Avenue) after
a particularly frustrating outing with one or more of us kids.

14TH ST.

S. 4TH AVE.

Fiddlesticks!

It's all gone haywire.

Go pound sand.

According to the Urban Dictionary, the origin of this saying derives from the longer expression, "He (she) doesn't have enough sense to pound sand down a rathole." Filling rat holes with sand was menial work, so an invitation to pound sand was not a compliment to the recipient. It dates to the early 1900s and is widely used in the midwestern United States.

Where was I when the lights went out?

Go fry ice.

"God help us and save us!" said Mrs. O'Davis as she fell over a peck of potatoes.

You're taking your half out of the middle!

She gets my goat.

Easy to get it, no fun when you do.

Don't turn up your nose at something you haven't tried.

Get off your high horse.

She'd be late for her own funeral!

If you don't like it
you can lump it.

You can't win for losing.

There's not room
for two kittens to dance!

It's all gone to hell
in a handbasket.

GET ON with it!

inertia, meet alacrity

"She'll be at it 'til the cows come home."

Drive it or park it!

Slower than molasses in January.

She has more excuses than Carter has pills.

Middle America in the mid-20th century: Saturday afternoon television consisted mostly of amateur talent shows, hokey musical programming, and other unassuming entertainments for the hard-working. All seemed to be sponsored by products like *GERITOL* (tonic), *CAMPHO-PHENIQUE* (antiseptic), *SERUTAN* (laxative) and *CARTER'S LITTLE LIVER PILLS* (headache, constipation, dyspepsia, and biliousness). The pills, as the name implied, were tiny, with many to the bottle and many bottles sold, hence "More _____ than Carter has pills."

Let's get crackin'!

The Oxford English Dictionary dates the expression "crack along" (to move briskly) from as long ago as 1541. According to research, "get cracking" first appeared in print in *Partridge's Dictionary of Slang & Unconventional English* in 1937. Some have speculated that "cracking" might also refer to cracking a whip—another reliable way to inspire brisk movement.

You're going all around Robin Hood's barn.

Where there's a will, there's a way.

There's no time like the present.

That'll happen when hell freezes over.

The road to hell is paved with good intentions.

Procrastination is damnation.

Come hell or high water.

Meaning *to succeed no matter what*, this expression came into its own in the USA. The first printed reference appeared in an Iowa newspaper, *The Burlington Weekly Hawk Eye*, dated May 1882: "The devil had broke loose in many parts of the country and, keeping up with the old saying, we've had unrevised hell and high water, and a mighty heap of high water, I tell you."

He's got no gumption.

Note: The first cousin of *gumption* is *moxie*.

He who hesitates is lost.

RALLYING CALLS

CALLS

strraighten up & fly right

"Take it away, Rosedale! "

In the early 1940s, NBC picked up and distributed nationwide a radio program originally called *Ezra's Barn Dance*. It was renamed *Uncle Ezra's Radio Station* and featured country music laced with homey talks and ficticious local news. The purveyor of these perky interludes was Uncle Ezra, broadcasting from his "powerful 5-watter" radio station E-Z-R-A in Rosedale, Illinois. He would be introduced by an announcer who would call, "Take it away, Rosedale!," at which time Uncle Ezra would rush in and ask breathlessly, "H'ain't missed nuthin' — have I?"

Damn the torpedoes, full speed ahead!

Front and center!

Let's show some vim and vigor.

Now, that's the spirit that won the war.

Lickety-split!

Another expression of American origin, likely by way of Scotland, "Lickety" is taken from the Scottish "lick," meaning speed, as in "going at quite a lick." The addition of "split," almost certainly the American contribution, adds rhythm, intensity, and yes, onomatopoeia. The phrase first appeared in American publications of the 1840s.

That's right up your alley.

Make hay while the sun shines.

NOW we're cooking with gas on the front burner.

Turn off the lights, and save the juice.

Faster than you can say, "Jack Robinson."

WHIMSY

but what does it mean?

"She thinks she's the cat's pajamas."

The urban United States of the 1920s and 30s was a motherlode of hipster slang. Young men and women flauted convention by donning daring ensembles, including the scandalous pajama. So the "cat" in this expression refers not to *felis catus* but to the androgenous *hepcatus* of the Jazz Age.

Every once in a blue moon.

Heavens to Betsy!

Whole books have been written about this and similar old-fashioned idioms. See also "Oh, my stars and buttons".

I'm tickled pink.

Oh, my stars and buttons!

The original expression, "Oh, my stars and garters!" referred to the highest heraldic order that a British monarch can bestow, *The Noble Order of the Garter*. The trade of garters for buttons may well have been my mother's invention, to avoid reference to what might be considered a titillating ladies' undergarment.

The bee's knees.

Originally meant to identify a thing absurdly insignificant, this phrase quickly morphed into meaning something achingly adorable. Other examples of the transformation: the flea's eyebrows, the canary's tusks, the kipper's knickers.

Cute as a bug's ear.

HEAVENS!

recognition of a higher authority

" He deserves a
front-row seat in heaven. **"**

The Lord only knows, and
He won't tell.

Saints be praised!

Thank the Lord and
all the saints.

Thanks be to God and
the Knights of Columbus.

That's all there is,
and there ain't no more.

except for the memories.

My mother's favorite poem

As I sat by my window last evening
The letter-man brought unto me,
A little gilt-edged invitation.
Saying, "Gilhooley, come over to tea."

Sure, I knew 'twas the Fogartys sent it,
So I went just for old friendship's sake.
But the first thing they gave me to tackle
Was a slice of Miss Fogarty's cake.

There were cloves, there was nutmeg and berries,
Rasins, citron and cinnamon, too.
There was sugar and peppers and cherries
And the crust of it nailed on with glue.

Miss Mulligan wanted to try it,
But really it wasn't no use,
For we worked on it over an hour,
And couldn't get none of it loose.

Till Murphy came in with a hatchet,
And Kelly came in with a saw.
That cake was enough, by the powers,
To paralyze any man's jaw.

Miss Fogarty, proud as a peacock,
Kept winking and blinking away,
Till she flipped over Flanagan's brogans
And spilt a whole brewing of tay.

"Aye, Gilhooley," she cried, "you're not eating,
  Take a little bit more for my sake."
"Oh, no, Miss Fogarty," says I,
"But I'll take the receipt for that cake."

McNulty was took with the colic,
McFadden complained of his head,
McDougal fell down on the sofa
And swore that he wished he was dead.

Miss Martin went in to hysterics,
And there she did wriggle and shake,
While everyone swore they were poisoned
From eating Miss Fogarty's cake.

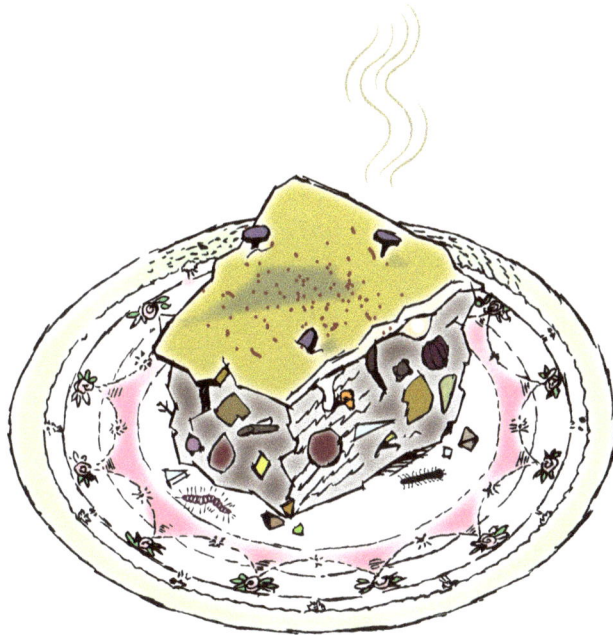

– Anonymous

about the author

ROBERT ROWELL is an accomplished classical pianist, finance and administration manager, cook, and *bon vivant*. He resides in San Francisco, California.

about the illustrator

SABETH IRELAND departed art school in Memphis, Tennessee and immigrated to San Francisco, where she acquired a degree in Technical Illustration. Ultimately, she returned to the visual arts by way of Graphic Design. She now lives in Amador County, California.

www.ingramcontent.com/pod-product-compliance
Lightning Source LLC
Chambersburg PA
CBHW060752150426
42811CB00058B/1383